**My Yoga Workbook: Mindful Bedtime Habits**

By: Lara Hocheiser and Nafeeza Hassan

Illustrated by: Nafeeza Hassan

International Standard Book Number 978-1-68418-145-2

# ABOUT THIS WORKBOOK

**Hi Kids! This yoga workbook was created for you!**

It contains many activities that will help you develop lifelong healthy habits. The activities will help you establish a bedtime routine so that you are rested. When you are well-rested, it's easier to think, manage your behavior, and make good decisions. It's also better for your immune system when you get lots of sleep. You may notice your overall health improves as you learn to include these activities in your bedtime routine.

You may also choose to do other things to help you get ready to rest at night. You can: put on cozy clothes, turn on gentle lighting, put on soothing music, remove all devices and things with screens from the room you are in, turn off notifications on all devices, roll out your yoga mat and get your mind and body in the mood to relax.

The activities will help you learn how to pay attention to what you are doing in the moment. Paying attention with curiosity and gentleness is also called being mindful. Breathing, doing poses, focusing, being mindful, relaxing, and reflecting are all part of your yoga practice. Yoga is always a practice. You never finish the practice. You just keep practicing and getting to know yourself better.

The words in this book could be tricky for you.
If you need help, please ask a grown up.

Please remember to only do the activities that feel right for you. If something hurts, you can stop. Listen to your body. It is very smart.

## This workbook belongs to:

```



```

# What will you find in this workbook

 **Time for Breath:** Taking your time to notice your breath helps you relax. Deep breaths can help focus the mind and bring you back to the present. Try the breaths in this workbook anytime you feel stressed or frustrated.

 **Time for Poses:** This book contains yoga poses you can cut out and do anywhere. Can you remember them in order?  Challenge yourself to do each pose slowly for 10 breaths. Relaxing and breathing in each pose will help you to wind down.

 **Time for Literacy:** Alone or with help, read the story. Use the poses during the story to bring it to life. Make reading fun!

 **Time for Focus:** Doing the focus activities will help you to focus your mind on one thing at a time. It's okay to get distracted, and when you do, gently bring your attention back to the activity.

 **Time for Mindfulness:** In this section, learn how to focus on what's going on right here and now. By being present in the moment, we can understand our feelings.

 **Healthy Habits:** Keeping track of your healthy choices will help you to build lifelong healthy habits. Try keeping track of the activities you do from this workbook for 4 weeks. As you keep track of your healthy habits, notice if relaxing at night becomes more pleasant. You may find you start to look forward to bedtime.

 **Time for Reflection:** How did the practices make you feel? Can you think of a time you could use the practice in your life? Take this time to reflect and wind down your day.

 **Time for Community:** Share the activities and practices from this workbook with the people you love. You are a teacher!

I LOVE...

MY NAME...

MY AGE...

FAVORITE THING TO DO BEFORE BED...

MY FEELINGS...

FAVORITE DREAM...

I WANT TO...

FAVORITE BEDTIME BOOK...

# LET'S MOVE!

**Practicing yoga before bed relaxes your body and mind before bed.** Set the mood for yoga. This will help you focus!

## Step 1:

Make the room comfortable for yoga.

- Put away any toys or objects that might be in your way.
- Put away electronics that might distract you. Music is okay–we love listening to soothing music during bedtime yoga.
- Change into cozy clothes that are easy to move around in.
- Roll out your yoga mat.

## Step 2:

Start the yoga sequence.

- Tell your mind and body it's time to relax.
- Set your intention for your practice. Think to yourself: What am I about to do? What are my goals? Is it to calm down and relax? Or perhaps it's to stretch?
- Complete the poses using the yoga pose sequence cards. Use them in order or mix them up!
- Take deep breaths during each pose.

**Tip!**
Listen to your body. Be patient and go slow. If something doesn't feel right, you don't need to do it.

## Step 3:

Reflect on how yoga made you feel.

- Use your Daily Practice Journal to notice how doing these activities makes you feel.

## I feel supported.

# FISH

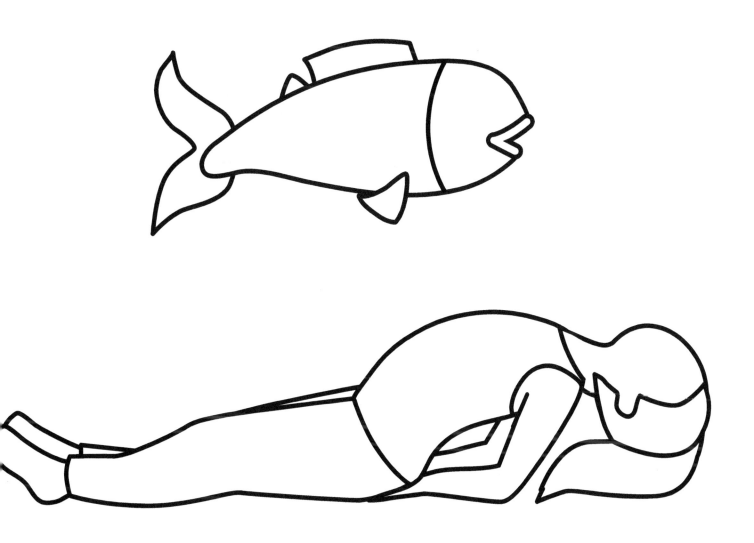

# My heart is open.

TIME FOR POSES

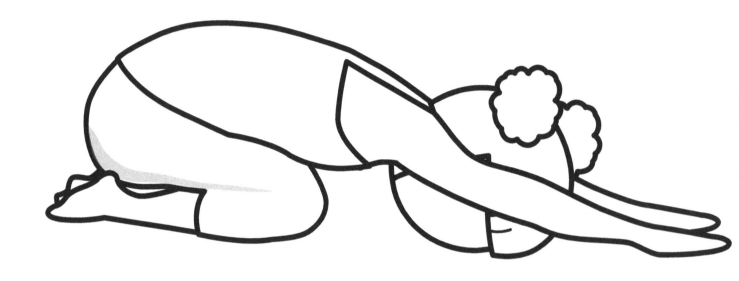

## I am connected.

## Symmetry balances me.

## I can let go.

**On the following pages, enjoy our yoga pose sequence cards.**

Cut the cards out so you can enjoy them anywhere. You can do them in order or change the order. You can challenge yourself to try to remember them in order and even make a game of it. Can you remember them in the reverse order, too?

**Play a game!** Shuffle the cards, draw one and act out the yoga pose or teach the yoga pose to a friend or a family member.

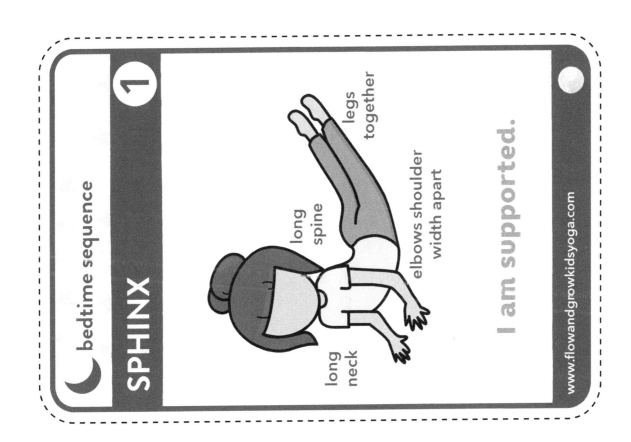

## bedtime sequence

### SPHINX

**1**

1. Lying on your belly, place your elbows under your shoulders.
2. Press down into both elbows, all your fingertips, your hips, and the tops of your feet.
3. Notice how doing so helps you feel supported by the ground.
4. As you press into the floor, grounding down, lift your heart forward and up. Lengthen your neck and move it in any way that feels comfortable.

*Note:* this pose is a modification of the Cobra pose, with elbows under shoulders.

**Optional Activity:**
Stay in Sphinx pose and allow your neck to move in ways that feel good. Stretch the front, back and sides of your neck by moving in a way that feels comfortable for you. You might choose to close your eyes.

www.flowandgrowkidsyoga.com

# YOGA POSES
# BEDTIME SEQUENCE

TIME FOR POSES

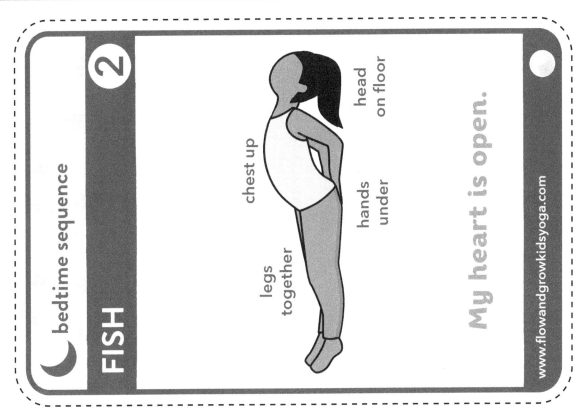

**bedtime sequence**

**2**

**FISH**

chest up

legs together

head on floor

hands under

My heart is open.

www.flowandgrowkidsyoga.com

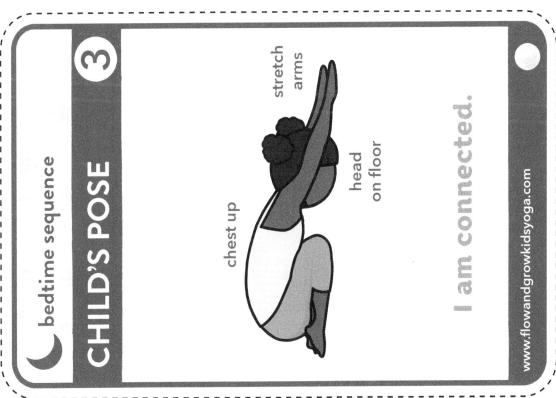

**bedtime sequence**

**3**

**CHILD'S POSE**

stretch arms

chest up

head on floor

I am connected.

www.flowandgrowkidsyoga.com

## bedtime sequence

## FISH  2

1. Sit down on your bottom with your legs extended in front of you.

2. Place both hands behind your hips and carefully place your elbows down on the floor on both sides. Try to bring your elbows in so they are under your shoulders.

3. Press your elbows into the floor as you lift your heart up.

4. Shine your heart toward the ceiling. If it feels right, let your eyes begin to look up. If it feels comfortable, you can begin to look back.

5. If your neck feels safe, you can let your head drop to the back. When you are done, carefully tuck your chin in toward your heart to lift your head again.

### Optional Activity:

Once you get your body into fish pose, try it with your legs in crisscross. How does it feel? Which version of fish pose do you like better?

www.flowandgrowkidsyoga.com

## bedtime sequence

## CHILD'S POSE  3

1. Start on your hand and knees.

2. Press your hips toward your heels.

3. Stretch your arms and heart forward and down into the ground. At the same time, keep your hips back and down toward your feet.

4. Breathe deeply and relax.

5. When you feel done, come out again.

### Optional Activity:

Keep your hips heavy in child's pose and then walk your hands over to one side. Drop your side down even more to stretch your entire side. Take a few breaths then switch to the other side. Does this variation of child's pose feel more challenging? What body parts feel like they got stretched?

www.flowandgrowkidsyoga.com

**4** bedtime sequence

**BOUND ANGLE**

spine & torso straight

hold feet together

long neck

Symmetry balances me.

www.flowandgrowkidsyoga.com

**5** bedtime sequence

**LEGS ON THE WALL**

arms & head on floor

extend legs

hip against wall

I can let go.

www.flowandgrowkidsyoga.com

## bedtime sequence

### BOUND ANGLE ④

1. Sit up tall with the bottoms of your feet together and knees bent wide.
2. If it feels okay for you, begin to fold forward. Stop folding wherever your body wants to stop.
3. Relax your eyes. When you feel ready, sit up tall again.

**Optional Activity:**
Do the pose upright and then try it again, allowing yourself to forward fold. Did you notice if one variation of the pose was more relaxing?

www.flowandgrowkidsyoga.com

## bedtime sequence

### LEGS ON THE WALL ⑤

1. Take a seat with your hip against a wall. Lay back and swing both legs up so your body looks like a capital letter L.
2. If this is too much stretch for your hamstrings (the backs of your thighs), scoot your hips back from the wall more so your knees can bend a little.
3. Close your eyes and enjoy.

**Optional Activity:**
Keep your hips by the wall and bend your knees. Allow the soles of your feet (the bottom part of your feet) to touch. Notice how this variation feels in your hips and back. Which variation was more enjoyable?

www.flowandgrowkidsyoga.com

# WHY DO I NEED SLEEP?

## Think about a time when you didn't get enough sleep.
How did you feel? Did you feel tired, groggy or cranky?

> ✏️ *Write about how it made you feel.*

We all need **sleep** and a good night sleep keeps you energized and focused! Just as a car needs to fill its tank up with gas, we fill up our own "gas tank" with sleep. Think about a time when you had a busy day and you felt exhausted. It's time to refuel!

## Why do I need sleep?
Our bodies and brains need rest. Most of us need about 9-12 hours of sleep to be fully rested.

Sleep helps regenerate our bodies and keeps our immune system strong! Did you know sleeping also helps us grow?

With enough sleep daily, we become our best selves. It can improve our memory, mood and focus!

# MINDFULNESS

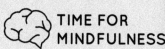 

## Mindfulness means paying attention with kindness and curiosity in the moment.

Our minds can be filled with many busy thoughts. Take the time to use your five senses to experience being in the moment. By clearing the clutter in our minds, we can become calm and aware of our surroundings—inside and out.

Take the time to become aware of your surroundings. With mindfulness, you can focus on one thing at a time instead of letting your mind wander off.

If you're being mindful around bedtime, pay attention to what you do. Choose activities that will help your brain and body relax.

## Practicing mindfulness takes time!

Use your senses one at a time. Take a deep breath, focus your attention, and ask yourself:

What do you see?  _____

What do you hear?  _____

What do you smell?  _____

What do you taste?  _____

What do you feel?  _____

# BOUND TO NOTICE

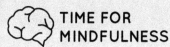

**TIME FOR MINDFULNESS**

**Mindfulness means focusing on what's going on right here and now.** In this activity, let's try this pose to calm your mind and stretch your hips and legs–the Bound Angle pose.

First, sit upright with your bottoms of your feet together and knees bent wide. Close your eyes, and then open slowly. Take a scan around the room and notice what is around you.

- What do you see with your eyes?
- What do you hear inside the room?
- What do you hear outside of the room?
- What do you smell around you?

Next, do the pose again, allowing yourself to forward fold as far as your body is comfortable. Spend a little time folded forward. Close your eyes. Now, take a scan of your body and your thoughts.

- What are your inner feelings?
- How does this pose feel?
- What do you notice about your inner thoughts?
- Can you hear anything inside your own body?

 *Use this space to reflect on this activity.*

---

*My Yoga Workbook: Mindful Bedtime Habits*

# BEDTIME AND ME

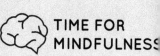

**Being mindful about your activities before bedtime can calm and soothe you to get a good night's sleep.** You can be your best self when you get enough sleep!

Get comfortable! Put on comfy PJs, get out your favorite blanket, whatever makes you comfy!

Create a bedtime routine and repeat it daily.

Turn off electronics such as cell phones and TV about an hour before bed.

Avoid caffeine and late night eating.

Exercise regularly! Try out the yoga poses in this workbook.

# BEDTIME ROUTINE

**What is a bedtime routine and why is it important to create one?** A bedtime routine is all of the things you do before going to bed. Think about some things you do before bed, such as, brushing your teeth, putting on your pajamas, or reading a bedtime story. All of these things form a routine and with daily practice, a consistent routine will make falling asleep easier, help keep you sound asleep and feel more energized in the morning!

✎ **Draw activities that you do before bed:**

| | | |
|---|---|---|
| **Brush my teeth** | **Put on pajamas** | **Read a story** |
| | | |

# BEDTIME ROUTINE

**TIME FOR FOCUS**

**List 5 things you do before bed.** On the left, write an activity that helps you wind down before bed. On the right, reflect on how that activity makes you feel. Does it make you happy? Why do you do this activity?

| ACTIVITY | FEELING |
|---|---|
| 1. | |
| 2. | |
| 3. | |
| 4. | |
| 5. | |

 **Optional Activity** .................................................................

Let's think about some things that make it hard to get ready for bedtime. Before sleeping, what are some things you may do that would make it hard to rest? Watching a scary movie? Texting with friends? Eating a heavy meal? Drinking a lot of liquids? Working on your homework? Can you think of more?

# BEDTIME COMPASSION

**Imagine sending compassion, love and gratitude to yourself and others.** Before going to bed, say a few words to send to your loved ones. It can even be something happy that happened to you today. Make this a routine that helps you fall asleep with love and gratitude.

First, think back on your day:

- Today, I felt _____.
- Today, I am thankful for _____.
- Today, _____ made me happy.
- Today, _____ made me peaceful.
- Today, I showed kindness by _____.
- Today, I showed gratitude by _____.

Then, send compassion to others:

- I send love to _____.
- I send gratitude to _____.
- I send kindness to _____.
- I wish sweet dreams for _____.
- I hope _____ has a great day tomorrow.

# BOX OF WORRIES

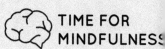

## Do you ever worry about things before going to bed?

It's okay to feel that way. If you find that your mind is filled with anxious thoughts before bed, try making a Box of Worries to put away all of your worries.

### Materials:

- Empty box with lid (or even a jar)
- Sheets of paper
- Art materials (such as crayons, markers, sequins, ribbons, pom-poms, construction paper, etc.)
- White paper, cut into strips
- Scissors

### Instructions:

1. Take an empty box and decorate it however you'd like! Add ribbons, pom-poms, or paint it–use your creativity. This will be your Box of Worries.

2. During bedtime, do you have any worries? If so, take a strip of paper and write or draw your worry. If you feel comfortable, talk about it with someone.

3. Fold up your worry and put it in the box. Once all of your worries are in the box, put the box away in a safe place. You can let go of these worries for now.

4. Whenever you're ready–it could be the next day or the following week, open your box of worries. Pull out a worry and ask yourself, "Do I still worry about this?" If you don't, remove it from the box and throw it out. If it still worries you, place it back in the box and if you feel comfortable, talk about it with someone.

# MOMENT FOR BREATH

**When we breathe, we take in oxygen which nourishes and provides energy for our body. Deep breathing can help calm and manage your emotions.**

Think about times where your breathing has increased. When you are upset or frustrated, do you notice that your breathing gets faster? Or when you are very excited—what is your breathing like? What about when you're scared? Notice how your breath is linked to your emotions.

Next time you are feeling uneasy or anxious, try taking control of your breath. By being mindful of your breath, you can manage your feelings. Remember: pause, take a deep breath, and be mindful about your next action. Breathing can help us make better decisions!

**When you feel anxious, uneasy or worried, try this breath.** Start with a point of the star to *breathe in* and then use your fingers to trace the star while breathing in and out.

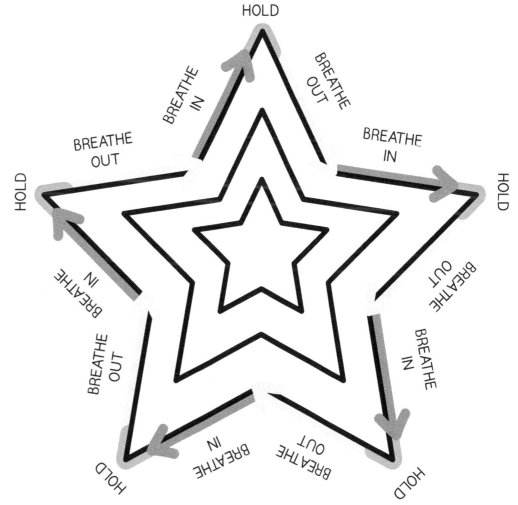

# MUDRA

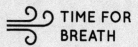 

**A mudra is a yoga pose for your hands.** Certain types of breathing give us the ability to feel calmer and more relaxed. Breathing enables us to check-in with our emotions and to be mindful of the moment. Try this breathing mudra in a quiet environment if possible.

## How To:

1. As you inhale, connect your thumb and pointer finger.
2. As you exhale, connect your thumb and middle finger.
3. On your next inhale, connect your thumb and ring finger.
4. On the next exhale, connect your thumb and pinky finger.
5. Repeat several times until you feel complete.

✏️ **How did this activity make you feel?**

*I inhale courage, I exhale negative thoughts.*

🧩 **Optional Activity** ..................................................

After you have done the breathing using the mudra several times, consider adding a word or a phrase to the inhale and exhale. The word or phrase for your inhale should represent something you want more of in your life, such as love or kindness. The word or phrase for your exhale should be something you'd like to let go of, such as negative thoughts about yourself. As you inhale and exhale, feel yourself bringing in what you need, letting go of what you don't. Notice how your heart, mind, and body feel when you're done.

# TEDDY BREATH

**Rock your teddy to bed with this relaxing breath.** Try this breath before going to bed. Find a quiet environment if possible.

## How To:

1. Lay down comfortably on your back. Place your teddy bear on your tummy.
2. Inhale deeply for three seconds. Watch your teddy rise up on your tummy.
3. Exhale deeply for four seconds. See your teddy fall as your tummy shrinks.
4. Do this for five-ten rounds.
5. How did it feel? Did you rock your teddy to sleep?

# 3-STEP MEDITATION

**A meditation is a practice that can calm and clear your head, bringing you to peace.** Find a quiet environment. Avoid any distractions. Sit in crisscross apple sauce. If you feel comfortabe, close your eyes.

**Ring a chime or a bell.**
Listen to the sound entirely. What does it sound like?

**Take deep breaths.**
Switch your focus to your breath. Do you feel your chest expanding and collapsing?

**Practice a body scan.**
From the head down, can you feel the sensations through your body? Notice how your body feels, through your arms down to your legs and toes.

✏️ **Write three words on how this made you feel:**

---

# GUIDED IMAGERY

**Guided imagery:** Next time you are laying in bed, try this written meditation to help you relax. Ask a friend or grown up to read it out loud for you.

*Lie on your back.*

*If it feels right close your eyes.*

*Bring your attention into your mind.*

*Notice if you have any thoughts.*

*Do you have a lot of thoughts? Racing thoughts?*

*Just a few thoughts? Loud thoughts?*

*Fluffy cloud thoughts?*

*Take a moment to notice what is in your mind.*

*Take a long pause.*

*Now imagine taking a large broom and sweeping your thoughts away, leaving the mind clean and clear.*

*Spend a moment visualizing yourself sweeping and tidying your mind clean of thoughts.*

*Rest another moment.*

**Short story:** Use this short story to put the poses together. Have a grown up or friend read it or read it yourself. Then, together or on your own, try the poses out.

Relax your mind and come on this bedtime journey.
Begin your journey in Egypt, a place of deserts and history.

You are walking past the **Sphinx** and notice the big open heart of the statue. What does this inspire in your own heart? You begin to warm up and decide to take a swim.

Now you are swimming down the Nile river with many **fish**. What sizes are the fish you see? What colors are they? Do they speak to you?

Now that night has fallen, you come back to land. You are lying on your back in **legs on the wall pose** and you look up and see the night moon.

You see a sleeping mouse in **child's pose** nestled behind some rocks. Are you beginning to feel cozy and sleepy too?

As you become ready to drift into sleep, you are back home. You whisper about your adventure to your teddy bear (**bound angle pose**). The two of you cuddle up and get ready for dreamland. *Good night!*

 **Follow-up:** Try to remember the order of the story. Retell it, or draw it.

**Challenge:** Make up, write or draw your own story using the bedtime yoga poses. Be as creative as you want.

# FILL IN THE STORY

TIME FOR LITERACY

**Make a silly story!** Fill in the blanks with a type of word asked for (noun, verb, place, etc.). After all of the blanks are filled, read the story out loud with a grown-up or friend!

.................................................................

The sun was starting to go _____. A _____boy yawned
                          DIRECTION              ADJECTIVE

and stretched his legs out. He was finished working on his _____
                                                                   NOUN

and it was time to put it away for the evening. Every night, the boy

started to unwind by doing _____, _____, and
                                  ACTIVITY              ACTIVITY

_____. He used to watch _____ before bed, but the
    ACTIVITY                              NOUN

bright lights kept him awake after bedtime. He felt _____ every
                                                           EMOTION

time he saw scary movies at night, which made sleeping _____.
                                                                ADVERB

He learned to practice _____ to begin to relax his body and mind.
                           BOOK ACTIVITY

His favorite nighttime yoga pose is _____, which he taught to his
                                         YOGA POSE

_____. The whole family learned about _____so now
  FAMILY MEMBER                                          NOUN

they practice it before bed. Going to bed used to be a chore, but now everyone

_____it. Doing yoga and winding down has made bedtime
    VERB

something to look forward to.

Good _____.
        TIME OF DAY

**Make a silly story!** Fill in the blanks with a type of word asked for (noun, verb, place, etc.). After all of the blanks are filled, read the story out loud with a grown-up or friend!

..................................................................................................

It was a _____ night. The moon was _____ and
          TEMPERATURE                                  ADJECTIVE

full. I could see the _____ castle peering beyond the Forest of
                                  SIZE

_____. We were on a top-secret mission to deliver the sacred
      NOUN

_____ to the castle.
      OBJECT

*"We need to go through the forest to get to the castle! Queen*

_____ *is counting on us!,"* chirped my best friend Robbie, the
      NAME

_____ parrot.
      COLOR

We traveled through the forest with a magical _____. The forest
                                          TRANSPORTATION

was wonderful! We saw a _____, and _____ and
                          ANIMAL                     PLANT

even a large _____ as big as a boulder! We finally came to the
                      FRUIT

end of the forest, where we met Slater the _____. Slater was the
                                      ANIMAL

guardian of the Forest Gate. He wore a _____ hat and bright
                                    ADJECTIVE

_____ glasses.
      COLOR

*"Who wishes to pass?,"* inquired Slater.

---

We explained our dire quest to him.

*"In order to pass the gate, you must beat me in a dance off!"* exclaimed Slater.

Challenge accepted! So I put on my favorite song, _____
                                                      **FAVORITE SONG**

and began to dance. For my finishing dance move, I performed my famous

_____.
**DANCE MOVE**

*"Wow, you have some _____ moves! You may pass the gate! Say*
                        **ADJECTIVE**

*the words, _____ to open the gate!"*
            **EXCLAMATION**

We made our way to the castle and delivered the sacred relic to the Queen. The

Queen threw us a huge party, filled with music and as much _____
                                                              **DESSERT**

as I wanted! We even played a game of _____ !
                                        **SPORT**

Then, I heard a loud _____. The sudden sound alerted me! I woke
                       **SOUND**

up, laying in my bed, wearing my favorite _____ pajamas. It was all
                                            **COLOR**

a dream...

**Color me!** A mandala is a circle that frames repeating geometric shapes. Enjoy coloring the following mandalas. Keep calm and focused.

**Color me!** A mandala is a circle that frames repeating geometric shapes. Enjoy coloring the following mandalas. Keep calm and focused.

# TRATAK EYE FOCUS

**A tratak is an eye exercise. Exercising our eyes can improve focus and attention.**

## How To:

1. Color the night scene on the next page. Make it your very own!
2. Once finished, place the coloring page on a table, desk or hang it up on a wall at eye level.
3. Practice moving your eyes slowly around the page.
4. First, start at the moon and stars on the top left.
5. Move your eyes down to the fish.
6. Move your eyes to the sphinx, then up to the mouse and back up to the moon.
7. Pause, blink a few times and take a deep breath.
8. Reverse directions.
9. Take a moment to reflect on what that was like for you. Do your eyes feel stronger? Do you feel focused?

✏️ **How did this activity make you feel?**

TIME FOR FOCUS

**Color me!** Can you find the matching night caps?

# NIGHT AND DAY BLANKET

TIME FOR FOCUS

# SLEEPING MOUSE MAZE

**Help the sleeping mouse get to bed!** Use a pencil, marker or crayon to solve the puzzle and reach the bed. *(Answer located on page 68)*

# SPOT THE DIFFERENCES

TIME FOR FOCUS

**There are 8 differences below!** Can you find them all?
*(Answers are located on page 68)*

# WORD SEARCH

**Find the words in the list below.** The words may appear horizontally, vertically, or diagonally. Can you find them all?
*(Answers are located on page 67)*

| Q | D | T | E | D | D | Y | B | E | A | R | B | Z | B | I |
| U | M | Y | V | M | U | D | R | A | K | U | C | W | E | F |
| K | D | S | C | M | F | I | S | H | Q | P | H | S | D | A |
| M | R | Q | G | N | B | I | L | X | L | S | I | A | T | C |
| W | D | A | O | Z | M | D | X | I | W | F | L | Q | I | T |
| V | E | O | O | X | S | W | D | Y | N | V | D | E | M | Z |
| V | M | G | K | W | B | P | M | H | J | X | S | H | E | D |
| X | R | W | Y | I | O | I | H | K | H | O | P | A | R | A |
| F | B | E | F | P | J | F | Q | I | U | G | O | U | G | A |
| U | B | G | S | E | T | T | S | L | N | T | S | U | T | R |
| R | L | R | Z | T | S | X | D | Y | M | X | E | R | A | Q |
| O | N | L | E | G | S | O | N | T | H | E | W | A | L | L |
| Y | P | T | O | Z | I | V | R | X | C | N | U | M | W | J |
| N | R | N | Y | K | B | Y | K | M | U | F | F | J | Q | O |
| W | P | H | Y | O | T | Y | S | S | P | L | F | O | C | B |

## WORD BANK:

Teddy bear

Bedtime

Egypt

Rest

Fish

Mudra

Childs pose

Moon

Sphinx

Legs on the Wall

 What did you dream about last night? _____

# CROSSWORD PUZZLE

TIME FOR FOCUS

**Solve the puzzle!** Use the clues below to answer the crossword puzzle. *(Answers are located on page 67)*

## ACROSS:

3. A mythical creature with the head of a human and the body of a lion
4. Celestial body that revolves around the Earth
5. At night when you are ready to go to sleep
8. A yoga pose, using the wall to make an 'L'
9. A plush toy, often resembling a bear

## DOWN:

1. Creature that lives underwater
2. A yoga pose that looks like a sleeping mouse
4. A yoga pose for your hands
6. Where you can find the Sphinx and Great Pyramid of Giza
7. Another word for relaxing

**The sleeping mouse is dreaming peacefully!** Use your imagination to draw the mouse's dream.

## Complete the teddy bear using the grid lines as a guide.

You might find it easier to copy one square at a time – the image is symmetrical (which means it's the same on both sides!).

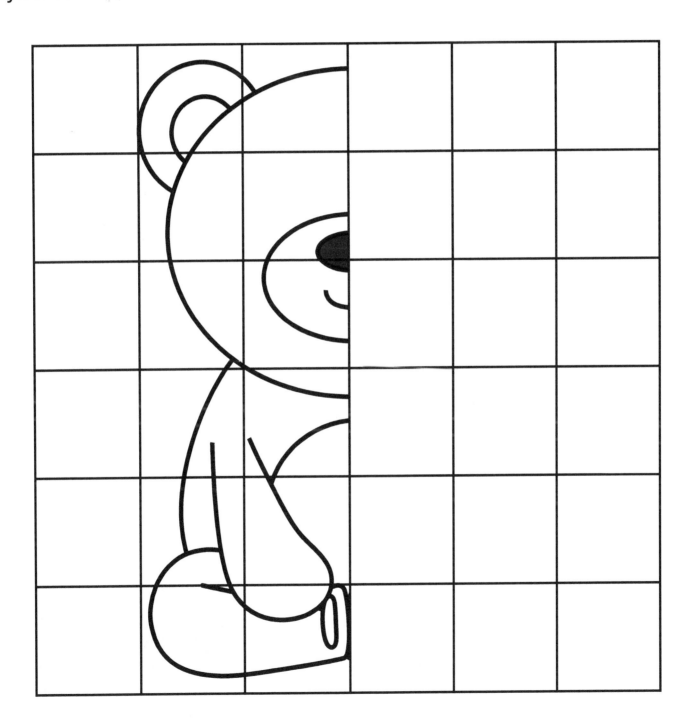

# SHADOW PUPPETS

TIME FOR FOCUS

## Make your own shadow puppets and tell a story!

1. Using a pair of scissors, cut out the shadow puppet shapes.

2. Then, with a piece of tape, attach a popsicle stick, straw, or pencil to the back of each shadow puppet.

3. Turn off the lights and use a flashlight or other light source to cast a shadow behind the shadow puppets.

4. Use your imagination to tell a bedtime tale!

# DREAMCATCHER

TIME FOR
FOCUS

**Make a dreamcatcher!** The Ojibwa Native American tribe believed in using dreamcatchers to catch bad dreams. It was believed that good dreams would slip through the center while bad dreams would be caught in the net.

1. Decorate your dreamcatcher, beads and feathers with markers and crayons.

2. Using scissors, cut out the dream catcher and beads.

3. With a hole punch, punch holes in the dreamcatcher and beads.

4. Then, tie pieces of string to hang the feathers and beads from the dreamcatcher.

5. Finish by tying a piece a string to the top of the dreamcatcher and hang your dreamcatcher next to your bed!

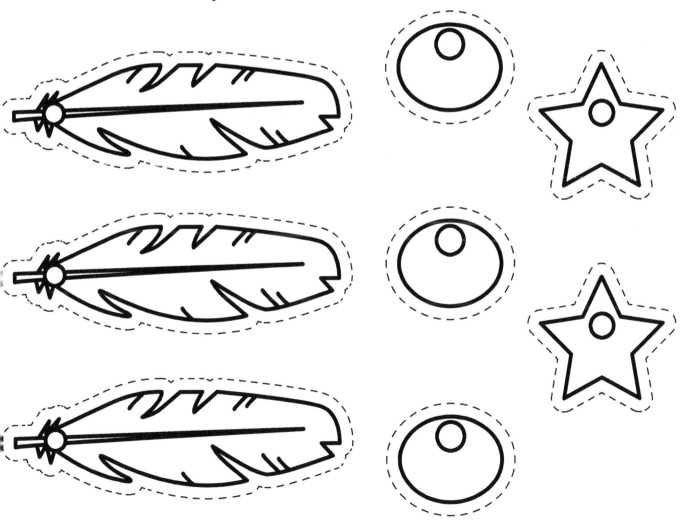

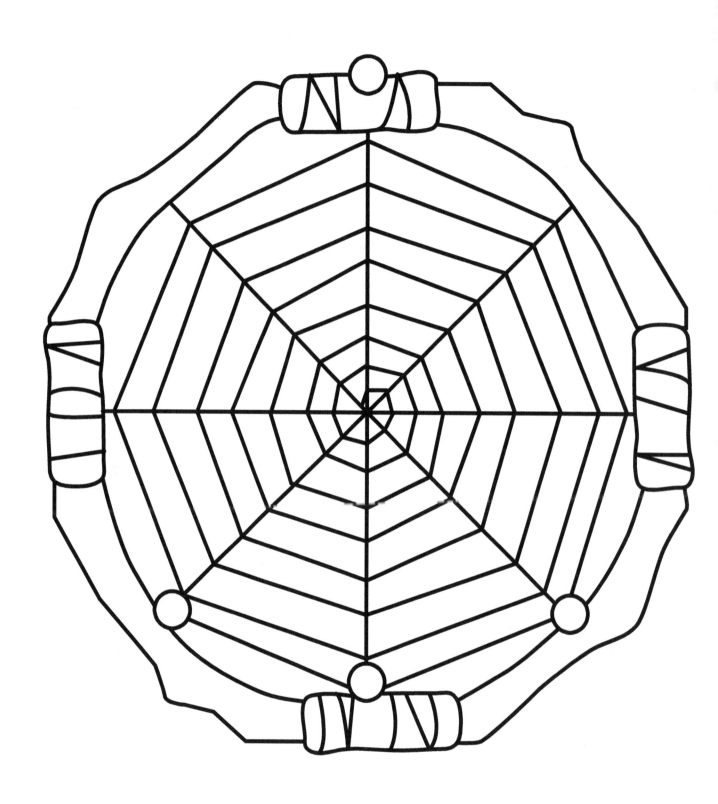

TIME FOR POSES

## Sphinx Pose:

1. Lying on your belly, place your elbows under your shoulders.

2. Press down into both elbows, all your fingertips, your hips, and the tops of your feet.

3. Notice how doing so helps you feel supported by the ground.

4. As you press into the floor, grounding down, lift your heart forward and up. Lengthen your neck and move it in any way that feels comfortable.

*Note*, this pose is a modification of the Cobra pose, with elbows under shoulders.

## Optional Activity ..............................................

Stay in sphinx pose and allow your neck to move in ways that feel good. Stretch the front, back, and sides of your neck by moving in a way that feels comfortable for you. You might choose to close your eyes.

## Fish Pose:

1. Sit down on your bottom with your legs extended in front of you.

2. Place both hands behind your hips and carefully place your elbows down on the floor on both sides. Try to bring your elbows in so they are under your shoulders.

3. Press your elbows into the floor as you lift your heart up.

4. Shine your heart toward the ceiling. If it feels right, let your eyes begin to look up. If it feels comfortable, you can begin to look back.

5. If your neck feels safe, you can let your head drop to the back. When you are done, carefully tuck your chin in toward your heart to lift your head again.

 ## Optional Activity ..............................................

Once you get your body into fish pose, try it with your legs in crisscross. How does it feel? Which version of fish pose does your body prefer?

# YOGA POSES BREAKDOWNS

TIME FOR POSES

## Child's Pose:

1. Start on your hand and knees.

2. Press your hips toward your heels.

3. Stretch your arms and heart forward and down into the ground. At the same time, keep your hips back and down toward your feet.

4. Breathe deeply and relax.

5. When you feel done, come out again.

 **Optional Activity**....................................................................................

Keep your hips heavy in child's pose and then walk your hands over to one side. Drop your opposite hip down even more to stretch your side body. Take a few breaths then switch to the other side. Did this variation of child's pose feel more challenging? What parts of your body feel like they got stretched?

## Bound Angle Pose:

1. Sit up tall with the bottoms of your feet together and knees bent wide.
2. If it feels okay for you, begin to fold forward. Stop folding wherever your body wants to stop.
3. Relax your eyes. When you feel ready, sit up tall again.

**Optional Activity**....................................................................................

Do the pose upright and then try it again, allowing yourself to forward fold. Did you notice if one variation of the pose was more relaxing?

# YOGA POSES
# BREAKDOWNS

## Legs on the Wall Pose:

1. Take a seat with your hip against a wall. Lay back and swing both legs up so your body looks like a capital letter L.

2. If this is too much stretch for your hamstrings (the backs of your thighs), scoot your hips back from the wall more so your knees can bend a little.

3. Close your eyes and enjoy.

 **Optional Activity**..................................................................
Keep your hips by the wall and bend your knees. Allow the soles of your feet (the bottom part of your feet) to touch. Notice how this variation feels for your hips and back. Which variation was more enjoyable?

## How did these poses make you feel?

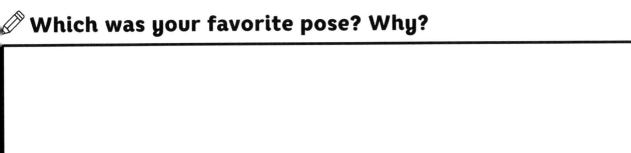

## Which was your favorite pose? Why?

# BEDTIME JOURNAL

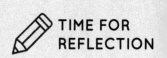

**Use this writing journal to reflect on activities you have completed in this book.** On the following pages, reflect on how keeping track of your healthy habits feels. Which daily practices were easy for you? Which ones were tricky? Did you enjoy the challenge of practicing on your own?

_____

_____

_____

_____

_____

_____

_____

_____

_____

_____

_____

_____

_____

_____

_____

# DAILY PRACTICE JOURNAL

HEALTHY HABITS

**Create healthy habits.** Tracking your choices in your daily practice journal is a way to create healthy habits. You will find that making healthy choices becomes easier with time. Keep track of your healthy choices here and after each day, reflect briefly on how it feels.

| | MON | TUES | WED | THURS | FRI | SAT | SUN |
|---|---|---|---|---|---|---|---|
| Time for Breath | | | | | | | |
| Time for Poses | | | | | | | |
| Time for Literacy | | | | | | | |
| Time for Focus | | | | | | | |
| Time for Mindfulness | | | | | | | |
| Healthy Habits | | | | | | | |
| Time for Reflection | | | | | | | |
| Time for Community | | | | | | | |
| | | | | | | | |
| | | | | | | | |
| | | | | | | | |

# DAILY PRACTICE JOURNAL

HEALTHY HABITS

| | MON | TUES | WED | THURS | FRI | SAT | SUN |
|---|---|---|---|---|---|---|---|
| Time for Breath | | | | | | | |
| Time for Poses | | | | | | | |
| Time for Literacy | | | | | | | |
| Time for Focus | | | | | | | |
| Time for Mindfulness | | | | | | | |
| Healthy Habits | | | | | | | |
| Time for Reflection | | | | | | | |
| Time for Community | | | | | | | |
| | | | | | | | |
| | | | | | | | |
| | | | | | | | |
| | | | | | | | |
| | | | | | | | |

# DAILY PRACTICE JOURNAL

HEALTHY HABITS

| | MON | TUES | WED | THURS | FRI | SAT | SUN |
|---|---|---|---|---|---|---|---|
| Time for Breath | | | | | | | |
| Time for Poses | | | | | | | |
| Time for Literacy | | | | | | | |
| Time for Focus | | | | | | | |
| Time for Mindfulness | | | | | | | |
| Healthy Habits | | | | | | | |
| Time for Reflection | | | | | | | |
| Time for Community | | | | | | | |
| | | | | | | | |
| | | | | | | | |
| | | | | | | | |
| | | | | | | | |
| | | | | | | | |

# DAILY PRACTICE JOURNAL

HEALTHY HABITS

|  | MON | TUES | WED | THURS | FRI | SAT | SUN |
|---|---|---|---|---|---|---|---|
| Time for Breath |  |  |  |  |  |  |  |
| Time for Poses |  |  |  |  |  |  |  |
| Time for Literacy |  |  |  |  |  |  |  |
| Time for Focus |  |  |  |  |  |  |  |
| Time for Mindfulness |  |  |  |  |  |  |  |
| Healthy Habits |  |  |  |  |  |  |  |
| Time for Reflection |  |  |  |  |  |  |  |
| Time for Community |  |  |  |  |  |  |  |
|  |  |  |  |  |  |  |  |
|  |  |  |  |  |  |  |  |
|  |  |  |  |  |  |  |  |
|  |  |  |  |  |  |  |  |
|  |  |  |  |  |  |  |  |

# DAILY PRACTICE JOURNAL

HEALTHY HABITS

|  | MON | TUES | WED | THURS | FRI | SAT | SUN |
|---|---|---|---|---|---|---|---|
| Time for Breath |  |  |  |  |  |  |  |
| Time for Poses |  |  |  |  |  |  |  |
| Time for Literacy |  |  |  |  |  |  |  |
| Time for Focus |  |  |  |  |  |  |  |
| Time for Mindfulness |  |  |  |  |  |  |  |
| Healthy Habits |  |  |  |  |  |  |  |
| Time for Reflection |  |  |  |  |  |  |  |
| Time for Community |  |  |  |  |  |  |  |
|  |  |  |  |  |  |  |  |
|  |  |  |  |  |  |  |  |
|  |  |  |  |  |  |  |  |
|  |  |  |  |  |  |  |  |
|  |  |  |  |  |  |  |  |

# DAILY PRACTICE JOURNAL

HEALTHY HABITS

| | MON | TUES | WED | THURS | FRI | SAT | SUN |
|---|---|---|---|---|---|---|---|
| Time for Breath | | | | | | | |
| Time for Poses | | | | | | | |
| Time for Literacy | | | | | | | |
| Time for Focus | | | | | | | |
| Time for Mindfulness | | | | | | | |
| Healthy Habits | | | | | | | |
| Time for Reflection | | | | | | | |
| Time for Community | | | | | | | |
| | | | | | | | |
| | | | | | | | |
| | | | | | | | |
| | | | | | | | |
| | | | | | | | |

# SHARE & REFLECT

**Share an activity from this workbook with someone special!** Once you've completed the activity together take a moment to write or draw or create a collage on this page to reflect how teaching and learning from each other felt.

## Word Search

```
Q   D   T   E   D   D   Y   B   E   A   R   B   Z   B   I
U   M   Y   V   M   U   D   R   A   K   U   C   W   E   F
K   D   S   C   M   F   I   S   H   Q   P   H   S   D   A
M   R   Q   G   N   B   I   L   X   L   S   I   A   T   C
W   D   A   O   Z   M   D   X   I   W   F   L   Q   I   T
V   E   O   O   X   S   W   D   Y   N   V   D   E   M   Z
V   M   G   K   W   B   P   M   H   J   X   S   H   E   D
X   R   W   Y   I   O   I   H   K   H   O   P   A   R   A
F   B   E   F   P   J   F   Q   I   U   G   O   U   G   A
U   B   G   S   E   T   T   S   L   N   T   S   U   T   R
R   L   R   Z   T   S   X   D   Y   M   X   E   R   A   Q
O   N   L   E   G   S   O   N   T   H   E   W   A   L   L
Y   P   T   O   Z   I   V   R   X   C   N   U   M   W   J
N   R   N   Y   K   B   Y   K   M   U   F   F   J   Q   O
W   P   H   Y   O   T   Y   S   S   P   L   F   O   C   B
```

## Crossword Puzzle

### ACROSS:

3.  A mythical creature with the head of a human and the body of a lion - SPHINX
4.  Celestial body that revolves around the Earth - MOON
5.  At night when you are ready to go to sleep - BEDTIME
8.  A yoga pose, using the wall to make an 'L' - LEGS ON THE WALL
9.  A plush toy, often resembling a bear - TEDDY BEAR

### DOWN:

1.  Creature that lives underwater - FISH
2.  A yoga pose that looks like a sleeping mouse - CHILDS POSE
4.  A yoga pose for your hands - MUDRA
6.  Where you can find the Sphinx and Great Pyramid of Giza - EGYPT
7.  Another word for relaxing - REST

## Sleeping Mouse Maze

## Spot the Differences

CPSIA information can be obtained
at www.ICGtesting.com
Printed in the USA
LVHW060401230719
624964LV00020B/1398/P